MIKE LEW

Mike Lew's plays include *Teenage Dick* (Donmar Warehouse, Ma-Yi at the Public, Wooly Mammoth, Huntington, Artists Rep); *Tiger Style!* (Olney, Huntington, La Jolla Playhouse, Alliance); *Bike America* (Ma-Yi, Alliance); and *microcrisis* (Ma-Yi, InterAct, Next Act). He and Rehana Lew Mirza are joint Mellon Foundation Playwrights in Residence at Ma-Yi Theater where they are co-writing *The Colonialism Trilogy* in addition to the book to the musical *Bhangin' It* with composer/lyricist Sam Willmott (La Jolla Playhouse, McCarter; Richard Rodgers Award; Project Springboard and Rhinebeck Writers Retreat workshops). Mike is a Dramatists Guild Council member, Tony voter, and New Dramatists resident. Honors: Lark Venturous and NYFA fellowships; PEN, Lanford Wilson, Helen Merrill, Heideman, and Kendeda awards. Education: Juilliard, Yale.

Mike Lew

TEENAGE DICK

NICK HERN BOOKS

London

www.nickhernbooks.co.uk

A Nick Hern Book

Teenage Dick first published in Great Britain in 2019 as a paperback original by Nick Hern Books Limited, The Glasshouse, 49a Goldhawk Road, London W12 8QP

Teenage Dick © 2019 Mike Lew
Introduction copyright © 2019 Mike Lew

Mike Lew has asserted his moral right to be identified as the author of this work

Cover photograph of Daniel Monks; Design: AKA

Designed and typeset by Nick Hern Books, London
Printed in Great Britain by Mimeo Ltd, Huntingdon, Cambridgeshire PE29 6XX

A CIP catalogue record for this book is available from the British Library

ISBN 97 8 184842 872 0

Introduction
Mike Lew

I first met my actor friend Gregg Mozgala in 2005 through Youngblood, the writers' group for playwrights under 30 housed at Ensemble Studio Theater in NYC. Gregg ended up acting in several of my short plays and we built up an immediate rapport. In 2007 he acted in my Youngblood short *The Roosevelt Cousins, Thoroughly Sauced*, in which he played a drunk FDR at a polio clinic in Georgia lamenting that his best days were behind him just prior to winning the presidency.

Gregg has cerebral palsy, and in many ways the advocacy he does on behalf of the disabled community dovetails with the work I do on behalf of artists of color; we've kept up an ongoing conversation over the years about our responsibilities to our respective communities as well as how to use our art to subvert stereotypes and push issues of representation forward. In 2012 Gregg started his own theater company called The Apothetae, which aims to examine the disabled experience. He wanted to kick things off by commissioning me to write a new play – an adaptation of *Richard III* set in high school called *Teenage Dick*. I mean the title alone! How could I refuse? I immediately said yes, then did no writing for a year. But I couldn't stand the thought of that title going to somebody else so I hurried up and finished a draft.

The year-long delay wasn't just idle procrastination. I was incredibly intrigued by Gregg's proposal but it also brought me a great deal of trepidation: why adapt *Richard III* as opposed to just doing another production of the original? It's not like I could ever improve upon Shakespeare! But our mutual commitment to examining disability in a contemporary context was key. Many able-bodied actors have approached the role of *Richard III* and used the character's disability as a means for displaying their acting chops. But few disabled actors have gotten the chance to take on the role. In this sense, the original play uses disability as both a thematic metaphor and (for the actor) some kind of 'acting challenge' – the disability is performative as opposed to an experience that's actually *lived*.

If we're to examine the disabled experience today, we have to both acknowledge and in some way disrupt our forebears. *Teenage Dick* is meant to take the most famous disabled character of all time and challenge Shakespeare's conception that Richard's disability makes him inherently evil. The play attempts to explode not only that old conception but also its condescending modern-day cousin: that all disabled people are a metaphor for transcendence. (For a good year, Gregg kept sending me clip after clip of American high-school sports teams smugly including a disabled classmate on their team in a blatant attempt at demonstrative inclusivity.)

I've actually grown to realize *Teenage Dick* is part of a whole subclass of new play adaptations that use existing works as a jumping-off point to disrupt the canon and make more room for marginalized groups. I'm thinking particularly of Branden Jacobs-Jenkins' *An Octoroon* (which re-appropriates Black stock characters from melodrama to redefine our contemporary understanding of Blackness), or David Adjmi's *3C* (which subverts the gay stereotypes from *Three's Company* and the golden age of sitcoms), or Jiehae Park's *Peerless* (which uses Macbeth's ambition as a pointed critique of the stereotypes around Asian overachievement). In these plays adaptation is a *subversive act*. By undermining the dominant stereotypes of a marginalized group we seek to re-center that group so that they are the tellers of their own stories. It's my hope that *Teenage Dick* takes all the drama and stakes of murderous monarchal succession and by cramming that into high school (which can also be life-or-death) we approach a contemporary resonance that a straightforward production of *Richard III* could never provide.

Between the play's first reading in 2013 (at Ma-Yi Theater in NYC) through its world premiere production in 2018 (with Ma-Yi Theater at the Public), the play went through developmental workshops and readings across the US: the

Public, the O'Neill, Oregon Shakespeare Festival, the Playwrights Foundation, the Lark, Florida Studio Theater, St. Louis Rep, and Hudson Valley Shakespeare Festival – in addition to receiving a Venturous Fellowship to mount the world premiere. Throughout all that time Gregg stuck with the play for nearly every reading, and so did Shannon DeVido in the role of Buck. We became like this traveling band doing readings every few months in another new city.

In effect I wrote Gregg and Shannon a bespoke play. Which was thrilling because earlier in my career I'd written with specific actors in mind but have never gotten the chance to see that impulse through by working with the same performers from conception all the way through production. It's also important to me that I got to write for Gregg and Shannon specifically because I'm an able-bodied writer representing a group I'm not part of; I clearly don't know all there is to know about disability, and it's a group that's incredibly vast and diverse anyhow. And while it's true the play's politics won't sit well with every disabled audience member and that performers shouldn't be responsible for 'fixing' a play's flaws or rubber stamping its politics, I can say that spending 5+ years fitting these particular roles to these two performers has lent a specificity to the roles that I haven't achieved in other plays and for that I'm incredibly grateful.

That tailoring process has actually continued with Daniel Monks and Ruth Madeley for the London premiere at the Donmar Warehouse. When Daniel was cast in the role, he made an incredibly generous offer: he'd be happy to play the role as-is (even though he doesn't himself have cerebral palsy), or if I'd be amenable to it he'd also be happy to discuss the details of his hemiplegia and how the role might be adapted to fit his physicality specifically. I leapt at the chance to further adapt the play around him, and we began a series of rather intimate and intensely political conversations around Daniel's life experience, leading to tweaks on several key passages. Heading into the London premiere I'm curious to see how these changes play out for the audience; in the same way there's a certain US–UK exchange going on around our collective interpretation of Shakespeare there's also an exchange going on around American vs British disability politics.

In the play's further life, to me the success of *Teenage Dick* will not just be about adding a new perspective on disability onstage (which I think is important because there's so few available); it will also be in the way that theaters interacting with this play will have to shake up their business practices. Because in order to produce this play you have to find and hire two disabled actors. You have to make sure your physical plant is accessible. You have to think about audience engagement in a whole different way. And you have to partake in conversations you might not be otherwise having around equity and access. My hope is that over the long-term *Teenage Dick* will be but one conversation-starter among a wide constellation of plays that give voice to disabled characters (written by able-bodied and disabled playwrights alike), and that in the process of dismantling its Shakespearean starter material we begin to dismantle our biases.

December 2019

A version of this article was first published in TheatreForum.

Teenage Dick received its world premiere by Ma-Yi Theater Company (Ralph B. Peña, Producing Artistic Director), on 20 June 2018, at the Public Theater, New York City. The cast was as follows:

RICHARD	Gregg Mozgala
BUCK	Shannon DeVido
ELIZABETH	Marinda Anderson
EDDIE	Alex Breaux
CLARISSA	Sasha Diamond
ANNE	Tiffany Villarin

Director	Moritz von Stuelpnagel
Set Designer	Wilson Chin
Costume Designer	Junghyun Georgia Lee
Lighting Designer	Miriam Crowe
Sound Designer	Fabian Obispo
Choreographer	Jennifer Weber
Production Stage Manager	Alyssa K. Howard

Teenage Dick was developed during a residency at the Eugene O'Neill Theater Center's (Preston Whiteway, Executive Director; Wendy C. Goldberg, Artistic Director) National Playwrights Conference in 2016.

Teenage Dick was developed by the Public Theater (Oskar Eustis, Artistic Director; Patrick Willingham, Executive Director).

Teenage Dick was commissioned and developed by The Apothetae (Gregg Mozgala, Artistic Director).

Teenage Dick was developed at The Lark Play Development Center, New York City.

Teenage Dick was developed with the support of Playwrights Foundation (Amy Mueller, Artistic Director), San Francisco, CA.

Teenage Dick received its UK premiere at the Donmar Warehouse, London, on 6 December 2019, with the following cast:

EDDIE IVY	Callum Adams
CLARISSA DUKE	Alice Hewkin
ANNE MARGARET	Siena Kelly
BARBARA 'BUCK' BUCKINGHAM	Ruth Madeley
RICHARD GLOUCESTER	Daniel Monks
ELIZABETH YORK	Susan Wokoma

Director	Michael Longhurst
Designer	Chloe Lamford
Lighting Designer	Sinéad McKenna
Sound Designers	Ben and Max Ringham
Video Designer	Andrzej Goulding
Choreographer	Claira Vaughan
Casting Director	Anna Cooper CDG

Characters

RICHARD GLOUCESTER, *male, seventeen, junior class secretary, slyly ambitious, has hemiplegia*
BARBARA 'BUCK' BUCKINGHAM, *female, seventeen, his best friend, earnest, wheelchair-user*
ELIZABETH YORK, *female, thirties–forties, wry, well-meaning English teacher, kind of naive*
EDDIE IVY, *male, seventeen, junior class president, football guy, kind of a dick*
CLARISSA DUKE, *female, seventeen, junior class vice-president, Jesus-loving, overachiever*
ANNE MARGARET, *female, seventeen, big-hearted yet dark, dancer, formerly the most popular girl in the school*

Setting

Roseland High School

Time

Now

This text went to press before the end of rehearsals and so may differ slightly from the play as performed.

Note

Cast disabled actors for Richard and Buck. They exist and they're out there.

To get a little more specific, Richard's character has a mobility disability; either hemiplegia (as was the case for the London production) or cerebral palsy (as was the case in NYC; see the back of this book for alternative lines specific to CP). Buck's character is a wheelchair user of unspecified etiology. For future productions, if there are disabled actors whose particular physicality doesn't exactly fit the above but would still make sense for the roles – go for it, this play is for you. But in no case should able-bodied actors 'play' disabled.

Scene One – Bare Stage

RICHARD. Roseland High School. Home of the Roseland Stallions.

Now that the winter formal gives way to glorious spring fling we find our rocks-for-brains hero Eddie – the quarterback – sleeping through his job as junior class president. 'Oh? Was I president? I've had so many *concussions* I must've forgot!' *Yeah.* He's Phoebus Apollo whereas I am but feeble. He makes sport of governance whereas I am not one who is shaped for sports.

I, Richard, am junior class *secretary*. Third in line behind Eddie the quarter-brains and Clarissa the goodie-goodie vice-president. *Welllll.* Maybe I can't play football, but I can run a play. The senior elections are upon us and from here I will vault past my inglorious station. Not by a pity vote. Not by campaigning. But by systematically destroying the competition. I'll take down Clarissa AND Eddie AND hold dominion over all of this school.

'But Richard,' you whimper. 'That's so so *mean*. Why would you wish for something so mean?' Because they all hate me, that's why! I was stamped for their hatred from birth. They see my unpleasant shape and like a magnet I must repulse, whereas *Eddie* draws in their adoration like so many iron shavings. Eddie who is naught but a Fabergé egg, all pretty surfaces hollowed of brains.

Well Eddie, dear egg, I will crack thee.
I come to *bury* Eddie, not to praise him.
Is this a ballot I see before me?
Eddie, the love I bear thee can afford no better term that this: thou art a douchebag.
(*School bell rings.*) Aw shit, I'm late for English. No matter. Watch this.

[handwritten margin notes:] Julius Caesar · MacBeth · Romeo & Juliet · "thou art a villian"

Light shift and we're in English class. RICHARD
approaches ELIZABETH.

Sorry I'm late Ms York. With my locker all the way across
campus it's so hard getting to class. You know, with my gait?

ELIZABETH. No worries, Richard! Have a seat.

RICHARD (*to audience*). Heh heh heh heh. (*He passes by*
BUCK.) What ho, Buckingham!

BUCK. Dirty Rich Yay-Ya!

They slap fives and RICHARD *sits.*

CLARISSA. Ms York? How come Richard gets to show up late
but when I'm late you read me the riot act?

ELIZABETH. Richard is different.

EDDIE. Differently *abled*? As in retarded?

ELIZABETH. Eddie don't use that word. What I *mean* is that
Richard is... well look at him Clarissa, he's got totally
differing needs.

CLARISSA. Buck has differing needs.

BUCK. Please don't involve me...

CLARISSA. And Buck always gets here on time.

RICHARD. Buck is on *wheels* you pox-scrabbled harlot. Do
I look like a race car to you?

EDDIE. Yo! Don't make fun of my lil buddy. (*To* BUCK.) You
cool, lil buddy, I got you.

RICHARD. *Whatever*. You're not even friends! Right Buck?

BUCK. Please don't... please don't involve me.

CLARISSA. It's kind of a double standard, that's all I'm saying.

ELIZABETH. Okay, you know what? Instead of everyone
telling me how to do my job let's see if you all did yours.
Machiavelli's *The Prince*. Did everyone read it? Buck?

BUCK. Uh-huh.

ELIZABETH. How about you, Eddie?

EDDIE. Like, a *thousand* percent.

ELIZABETH. Great. So then Machiavelli lists four pathways to power. Can anyone name me the first one? Yes, Richard.

RICHARD. The first pathway to power is fortune. Whether by being born into royalty or having a principality gifted to you, fortune is the easiest path.

ELIZABETH. Good! And the second?

RICHARD. Second is virtue. Through strength of character a prince may inspire in his *phalanx* a sense of *virile agitur* and *amor patriae*, thus creating *de novo* a principality *per angusta ad augusta*, which is by and by more impressive than inheriting an empire by fortune.

ELIZABETH. ...okay correct.

EDDIE. Dude: you're a FREAK.

RICHARD. Read a book, *Homo erectus*.

EDDIE. I'm def more erect than *you*.

RICHARD. Why, you've got a boner?

EDDIE (*vaguely threatening*). *Maybe*.

ELIZABETH. *Guys*. Can anyone tell me, Machiavelli's third pathway to power...

RICHARD. Civil election.

ELIZABETH. Richard let's give someone else a turn. Can somebody name me the fourth? Anyone. Did anyone else in here read words on a page and remember one word?

Nobody can.

(*To* RICHARD, *resigned.*) Okay, Richard, take it away.

RICHARD. The last pathway to power. Is *wickedness*.

ELIZABETH. *Yessss*. Bloody coup. Stabby stabby. Perfect Richard!

EDDIE (*mocking*). *Perfect Richard.*

ELIZABETH. I'm sorry, Eddie, did you have something to add?

EDDIE. No.

ELIZABETH. Then kindly shut up. Or better yet, answer this: What does Machiavelli say about whether it's better to be loved or feared?

EDDIE. Loved all the way.

ELIZABETH (*she does a 'wrong' buzzer sound*). What about you, Buck?

BUCK. Um. Feared?

ELIZABETH. Care to elaborate?

BUCK. No.

ELIZABETH. *Buck* you're my TA!

BUCK. I'm a shy TA.

RICHARD. Given a choice, it is best to be feared. For man is ungrateful, fickle, and greedy, and thusly being loved is a bond they may break. Whereas being feared is sustained by a dread of punishment that won't ever fail you.

ELIZABETH. Well I'm glad at least *one* of you is soaking up Machiavellian tactics for consolidating ABSOLUTE POWER – (*Echoing.*) power power power!

No response.

Okay did *anyone* else do the reading?

CLARISSA. I did the reading Ms York.

ELIZABETH. Clarissa, great!

CLARISSA. And I totally disagree with this assignment, from a religious and moral standpoint.

General groans.

ELIZABETH. Oh boy here we go...

CLARISSA. This book is telling me it's okay to lie and murder and steal, and all of that is really really cruel and totally goes against all of my Christian values.

ELIZABETH. Machiavelli was Christian. Machiavelli was Catholic.

CLARISSA. Whose work was banned by the Catholic Church.

ELIZABETH. Fine but *The Prince* isn't cruel, it's pragmatic. Machiavelli even speaks out against idle cruelty, because idle cruelty stirs people's hate.

RICHARD. I actually had a question about that.

ELIZABETH. Sure hon go ahead.

RICHARD. It's about that passage, on how not to be hated.

EDDIE. It's easy Dick. Talk less, shower more.

ELIZABETH. *Eddie.*

EDDIE. What? That's good advice! Matter of fact, I'm tweeting that. (*He tweets it.*)

ELIZABETH. No phones in here. Richard, go on.

EDDIE (*still tweeting*). His name isn't Richard, it's Dick.

RICHARD. That's not my name.

EDDIE. What's that *Twisty Dick*?

RICHARD. I said that's not my name.

EDDIE. Richard is a nickname for Dick.

ELIZABETH. Gentlemen.

RICHARD *turns around, hissing to* EDDIE, *all menace.*

RICHARD. I want you to know that this is the very best time of your life. It will *NEV*er get any better than this. The rest of your life will be spent searching in vain for this moment of former glory as your downward trajectory plunges you ever further from here.

EDDIE. I think I just pee'd a little.

ELIZABETH. Let's get back to the text. Richard, what was
your question?

RICHARD (*shaken*). Right... Machiavelli says cruelty is at
times warranted but that over-cruelty generates hate. But what
if you're hated to begin with? If cruelty is a viable tool then
why *stop* being cruel if you've always been hated since birth?

ELIZABETH. Jeez, I uh – Richard where is this coming from?

The bell rings. Everyone starts packing up.

Uh-oh, looks like that's an answer that'll have to wait. Okay
but everybody if we could just listen up for one second. Please
stop packing your bags. I just wanted to mention that as some
of you know I'm the faculty advisor for Class Council and that
speaking of civil election *senior elections* are coming up.
You all should think about running. Or re-running! Two years
in a row with Ms York! Whaaat?! *Woo-hooo party time. Untz-
Untz-Untz-Untz!*

CLARISSA *and* EDDIE *stare incredulously, then exit.*

BUCK. Hey buddyboy you coming to lunch?

RICHARD. In a minute. (*Direct address as* BUCK *exits.*) Pop
quiz, friends. What's the first step of staging a populist
uprising? Convincing the populace that they thought it up.
(*To* ELIZABETH.) Ms York? I'm so sorry for disrupting
class with my outburst.

ELIZABETH. Oh no, I should apologize for letting Eddie
mouth off. Does it affect your learning environment? We're
very sensitive to anti-bullying. If his comments verge on
bullying you let me know.

RICHARD. I'm fine. You're the one who's gonna have to deal
with him for a whole 'nother year.

ELIZABETH. Oh God, if I have to deal with that boy for
another term I'm gonna... I shouldn't say anything.

RICHARD. Go on.

ELIZABETH. I'm sick to death of these deadweights running our government! Richard, I don't know if you know this but being senior class president isn't just a ceremonial title. They have to ratify the student union fund!

RICHARD. *Really.*

ELIZABETH. Next year? The *football team* wants to secure the whole fund to install all-new bleachers. If that happens my poor drama-club students won't have any money left over for the school play. What are they supposed to do, buy their own sets and costumes? I know someone like you understands the importance – the all-consuming social importance of live theater!

RICHARD. I do.

ELIZABETH. Richard. *You* should run for president! Have you thought about running?

RICHARD. Not really.

ELIZABETH. But why? They elected you junior class secretary.

RICHARD (*suddenly dark*). Third in line. Yesss.

ELIZABETH. Granted you were running unopposed, but with all the experience you've accumulated? I think you'd have a real shot.

RICHARD. I doubt that. They all fucking hate me!

ELIZABETH. They don't f-word-ing hate you, don't say that! Who hates you?

RICHARD. Everyone! Everyone thinks I'm a freak! And it's not just my disability. Lookit me: I'm a virgin and I can't even drive.

ELIZABETH. Is that from *Clueless*?

RICHARD. That's from my life!

ELIZABETH. Richard did I ever tell you I had a brother who was disabled?

RICHARD. Did he have hemiplegia like me?

ELIZABETH. No he was... Down syndrome.

RICHARD. That's really not the same thing.

ELIZABETH. He was... He passed away a few years ago. But he was older than me? And I remember in high school. The other kids – just the cruelty.

RICHARD. Yo this is mad awkward.

ELIZABETH. Richard I'm just saying I get you okay? Now I know how you kids get super-emo with your moody music and your post-apocalyptic YA novels with all those maze-running kids and your sexy makeout vampire teams and your mockingjays...

RICHARD. What?

ELIZABETH. But I super-believe in you! We could redo the budget, slash wasteful spending, and save the arts!

RICHARD. Ms York, moved as I am to fructify your budgetary reseeding the electoral requirements seem... *awfully tedious.* I doubt I could even collect the two hundred signatures needed to run for office.

ELIZABETH. Oh no, don't worry about that. You can skip it.

RICHARD. *Really.* But if I'm hanging up posters I'll need more time to get to and from class.

ELIZABETH. I'll get you some hall passes.

RICHARD. What about the grade check? What if I'm below a B average?

ELIZABETH. Your grades are fine. And if they're not fine I'll talk to your teachers.

RICHARD. Ms York, if I ran for president, would you give me a driving lesson?

ELIZABETH. What?

RICHARD. Yeah, it's just… your belief in me is so inspiring. I've never been behind the wheel of a car because of my compromised motor skills. You do believe in me, right?

ELIZABETH. Hon, I drive a Dodge Durango. It's a big honkin' SUV. I can barely drive it. But focus on the election, okay? I really do think you could shake things up if you just take a chance!

Scene Two – Bare Stage

Seamless transition to…

RICHARD. Shake things up, yes. But by the time I'm finished with this baby it won't be a matter of chance. With my signature requirements waived I'm at leisure to run a covert campaign. After all, I could never beat Eddie out in the open. But you can't campaign against someone you don't know is running. Here from the shadows, I'll erode Eddie's base of support *and* engineer a major reversal in social standing. But is my social standing something I can even hope to reverse? (*Calling out.*) Buckingham. Barbara Buckingham. BUCK!

BUCK (*off*). YEAH WHAT?

RICHARD. A word with you sirrah.

BUCK (*enters*). Dude, what'd you call me? Stop talking like that.

RICHARD. I have a philosophical question.

BUCK. I love those go 'head.

RICHARD. Do you believe our social station is circummountable, or is it immutable?

BUCK. *Good question.* Immutable.

RICHARD. But… no, but don't you believe we can rise past our station, given sufficient cunning and skill?

BUCK. Nope no I don't. I'm not like you, yearning to fly beyond nature's boundaries like some kind of disabled nerd Icarus. Why do you ask?

RICHARD. No reason, Buckingham Buck-Barbie-B. It's just I've got plans for a date.

BUCK. A date? You? Who's gonna date *you*?

RICHARD. I was thinking of grabbing a date to the Sadie Hawkins Dance.

BUCK. Oh, I get it. You think by going to the dance you'll seem like less of a creepy renaissance-faire-talkin' weirdo...

RICHARD. And I'll rise past my circumstance, yes.

BUCK. *I like it*. I can help out if you want! Dyou wanna go with me to the dance? Not as a date or whatever but just like as friends?

RICHARD. Uhhh, I'll pass.

BUCK. Whatever jerkface, it's not like I *wanted* to be the matchy-matchy disabled couple.

RICHARD. That's fine.

BUCK. *That's fine??* You do know the Sadie Hawkins Dance is where the girl asks the guy out? I'm, like, the only girl who talks to you.

RICHARD. That's fine, I was actually thinking of going to Sadie Hawkins with Anne.

BUCK. Anne *Margaret*? But she's the most popular girl in school.

RICHARD. *Formerly* the most popular. Eddie broke up with her over winter break.

BUCK. So what? She's still super out of your league.

RICHARD. Is she Buck? Is she? Or maybe it's just that you don't know what league that I'm in.

BUCK....No, I'm pretty sure she's outta your league. She's hot, she's smart, she's super-talented. You know she's a quasi-professional dancer.

RICHARD. But now she's in wounded bird mode. If I can get her to ask me to the dance then I'll instantly vault past my inglorious station –

BUCK. Um, no ya won't.

RICHARD. – and for once other people might see me.

BUCK. Okay. If you had to ask Anne to the dance that would already be a humiliating rejection situation. But getting Anne to ask YOU? I mean what's your angle, hypnosis or cash? Plus why Eddie's ex-girlfriend? Is it a copycat thing? A revenge thing? A sex thing? A sex-revenge-copycat thing? Wait! Richard: is this a *scheme*?

RICHARD. What?

BUCK. You are always scheming. *Wait!* Richard: are you running for president?

RICHARD. WHAT?

BUCK. *Ommmiigooood.* Is getting a date with Anne Margaret the first step in some kind of elaborate, multi-step scheme for getting elected senior class president?? It is, isn't it. *CONFESSSSS.*

RICHARD. No, Buck! It's not a scheme, I just want a date.

BUCK. And I want Chris Evans to sit on my face. Only *he has to ask*.

RICHARD. Who's Chris –

BUCK. Chris Evans is Captain America, he's been Captain America in like *nineteen* movies. Do you even watch movies? Or are you too busy tuning in to the voices inside of your head?

RICHARD (*looking off*). Soft you now, she approaches.

BUCK. *Soft you now?* Who *talks* like that?

RICHARD. Away with you, Buck!

BUCK. Whatever pal. Follow your dreams. (*She exits.*)

RICHARD (*to audience*). Buck's right, of course. Landing a date with Anne Margaret IS part of an elaborate multi-step scheme. If I can capture Eddie's ex-girlfriend the people will know that I am a most redoubtable knave. Someone who's not to be *fuck-ed* with. And so: Roseland High School, prepare for your fate. My first step to power? Is to land a first date.

ANNE *enters*.

Hello Anne. I believe you had something to ask me?

ANNE. I did?

RICHARD. Uh-huh, so go 'head.

ANNE. I really can't think of anything. Can you get out of my way?

RICHARD. No, that's not it...

ANNE. I don't know what your deal is but I'm not into guessing games Richard.

RICHARD. This isn't a game, it's an invitation. So go ahead. Invite me to Sadie Hawkins. You just have to ask.

ANNE. Um, *excuse me*? Look, I know that you're differently *abled*, but you gotta know that's not happening.

RICHARD. But why Anne?

ANNE. Ummmm. Because I don't *like* you?

RICHARD. You don't even *know me*! You've known me since middle school and this is the most that we've talked.

ANNE. You're right, I *don't* know you. So why would I ask you out, cuz I pity you?

RICHARD. Nobody's asking for pity here. Why? Do you pity me?

ANNE. I...

RICHARD. Or do you fear me? Are you scared you might become paralyzed just by the taint of my touch? (*He touches her.*)

ANNE. Quit that!

RICHARD. See? You hate me for what I am.

ANNE (*fragile*). No I *don't*, I just… Richard, I don't mean to be mean, I'm just trying to stay in my lane here, ya know?

RICHARD. Which is it, Anne? Pity me, hate me, or fear me?

ANNE. I don't even know you. I *nothing* you.

RICHARD. *Exactly.* I'm not even relevant here. The real reason you're going to ask me to Sadie Hawkins is because it's the best way to get back at Eddie.

ANNE. *Eddie?* But I don't want to get back at Eddie.

RICHARD. *Really.* Even though Eddie was hardcore dating you up through winter break only to immediately start dating Liz Woodville.

ANNE. Eddie's dating *Liz*? No he's not.

RICHARD. Clearly you don't follow Liz Woodville on Instagram.

ANNE. …Whatever, it's done now, he can date who he wants.

RICHARD. I've seen you on campus Anne. Seen the happy-go-lucky social butterfly cocooning herself in a chrysalis of melancholy and doubt.

ANNE. Yeah, well, it's been a really hard year.

RICHARD. Which is why it's so brave of you soldiering on like this. You know something Anne? I've never known the tender pleasures of dating…

ANNE. Really.

RICHARD. …but then again I've never been unceremoniously *dumped.*

ANNE. That… that's – is that what people are saying?

RICHARD. That's right Anne. He's still the most popular person in school. Whereas you? You are nothing now.

ANNE. I'm not... I'm not *nothing*. I'm just me.

RICHARD. Being 'you' isn't enough. Not in this Roseland wasteland. If Eddie and Liz Woodville go to the dance, what's your counter-attack?

ANNE. Why do I even *need* a counter-attack? I swear to God, high-school drama's such bullshit.

RICHARD. Ask me to the dance. If you go with me, everyone will see what a good person you are. They'll see you did the selfless good deed of taking Richard – a cripple – to his very first dance. I'm your charm offensive.

ANNE. Okay but IF I did go with you, I'd only be doing it to be a good person. It doesn't mean we're, like, *dating*.

RICHARD. Not yet.

ANNE. Not ever!

RICHARD. Not ever... *yet*.

ANNE. God Richard, what kind of crazy fantasies go on in that head?

RICHARD. So many, Anne, you don't even know. So what's it going to be?

ANNE. Fine. Richard: will you go to Sadie Hawkins with me?

RICHARD....No.

ANNE. No?! You fucking *ass crack*.

RICHARD. No I can't go to the dance because I never learned how to dance.

ANNE. Well could I teach you, or something? I do have a dance background.

RICHARD. It's a date!

ANNE. Ah but it's not.

RICHARD. Ooooh. Spicy, Anne. 'Methinks the lady doth protest too much.'

ANNE. I think I'm protesting just right. (*She starts to exit.*)

RICHARD. Hey Anne?

ANNE. *Jesus*. WHAT?

RICHARD. *You're a good person.*

ANNE.... Thanks. (*She exits.*)

RICHARD. Ha! Did you fucking SEE that? ~~Was EVER a woman so easily won?~~ We're gonna be like Lancelot and Guinevere, Pyramus and Thisbe, Michelle and Barack! *Ohhh Buck?*

BUCK (*enters*). Hey, did you hear the good news? Eddie's running for re-election!

EDDIE (*enters*). I am running for re-election. (*He exits.*)

BUCK. He's so presidential. So commanding. Yet also approachable.

RICHARD. He's incompetent.

BUCK. Plus he's *super*-nice too, super-nice.

RICHARD. Super WHAT? Buck, the fuck are you talking about?

BUCK. Well he's always been nice to *me*.

RICHARD. Like that stunt he pulled with you at the Homecoming game? Carrying you on his shoulders for a symbolic touchdown??

BUCK. Exactly. That was a very nice gesture.

RICHARD. That was a PR stunt! The varsity squad was facing expulsion for hazing the JV team.

BUCK. Allegedly. You don't know! Those freshmen could've been broomsticking themselves.

RICHARD. So instead of prosecuting him for his sex crimes, he's all, 'Hey everybody, watch me get the football team to carry Buck. Lookit how nice we are to the *cripple*.'

BUCK. You can't call me that! You have fucking hemiplegia.

RICHARD. In the land of the cripples one leg is king.

BUCK. Screw you man, getting carried in for a touchdown was way fun.

RICHARD. Come on, admit that he used you!

BUCK. I mean... if a bunch of strapping lads wanna hoist me up and carry me like Cleopatra? Use me *all day*. Richard, don't be a cynic. If you're cynical *everything* looks like a cynical ploy. Whereas I choose to believe Eddie *tries* to be friendly.

RICHARD. *Friendly*. Right. (*Aside*.) And with middling friends like you, Caesar would've died of old age.

BUCK (*noticing him soliloquizing*). Are you... okay, we've gone to our happy place.

RICHARD. And yet! Eddie is not my only rival in this. Yes, it may feel like I'm playing *second* fiddle but by my troth I am woefully *third*.

BUCK. What are you...

RICHARD. Well fiddlesticks to the fiddler who fiddles about. If my pleas fall on deaf ears I'll change my tune. Buck?

BUCK. *Hey*.

RICHARD. Your spirited defense of our footballer-in-chief has swayed me entirely. Surely Eddie and I have our differences but he's not a bad chap. So if you support Eddie as I do, as clearly I as well do, what's to be done with the Clarissa situation?

BUCK. The what situation?

CLARISSA (*enters*). Clarissa for president! Vote Clarissa for senior class president.

BUCK. Oh that situation. Fuck me.

CLARISSA. Richard, Buck, hi! Hi, hi, hi! *Take a flyer*.

RICHARD. You're campaigning early.

CLARISSA. We are at WAR. Eddie can't just skate from election to election on a campaign of do-nothing handsomeness.

BUCK. Oh I'd say he can.

CLARISSA. Well he hasn't done *peep* for the junior class. I was that numbskull's vice-president all year and it made me wanna kick a bunny rabbit right in the teeth. I mean what are his policies? He's pitched that stupid wet T-shirt contest FOUR TIMES: as a special event, a fundraiser, a club, and a sport.

BUCK. Don't hate the player hate the fundraiser.

CLARISSA. I'm just saying we can beat him. We're not in some old-timey John Hughes movie with easily definable cliques. We can form a *coalition* you guys. The Christians, the Koreans, the Korean Christians, the theater weirdos, the marching-band rejects, you-you-you you guys.

RICHARD. You mean 'you guys' *the disabled*? You do know we're not some sideshow to your ascendancy.

BUCK. We're not a sideshow you shitshow!

CLARISSA. No I know that but –

BUCK. BOOOO. *Go away*. BOOOO.

CLARISSA. *No!* I'm just saying who cares about FOOTBALL. Who cares he's the quarterback? Who cares about his firm pecs and his sun-kissed skin and his soft hair and hard abs, his rock-solid abs…

BUCK. He's also a super-nice person.

CLARISSA. I'm a *nice fucking person*!! Look dudes, you gotta throw me a bone. If I don't get president I'll never get into Stanford.

RICHARD. And what about us?

CLARISSA. What about you? You'll probably get a full ride to whatever college you want. Because of your – Because you're. You know. Because of your…

RICHARD. *GPA?*

CLARISSA. No, because of your *legs*.

BUCK. And there it is. You are literally garbage inside of a sweater.

CLARISSA. You don't need the extracurriculars I do. College admissions are *dirty*.

RICHARD. So you're saying I have no right to this election. No need for it.

CLARISSA. *Sure you do*. Aren't you gonna run for, like, secretary again? Ooh you wanna be my campaign manager?

RICHARD. What if I wanted to be president. Would that be so CRAZY.

CLARISSA. *YES*. Richard, you know you'd never win.

RICHARD. Perchance. Perchance not by fortune, virtue, or civil election.

BUCK. Who TALKS like that? (*To* CLARISSA.) He's not running, he's just fucking with you.

CLARISSA. Well don't. We have to form a united front against Eddie and I NEED the freak vote, don't split that. You get it right?

RICHARD. Oh, don't worry. We know our place.

CLARISSA. Good. Good good good good! Here, take a pin. Buck, you can have a poster for your wheely-chair thing. Now let's Instagram your support.

BUCK. *No. No*. No Clarissa.

CLARISSA (*she takes a selfie with* BUCK *in it awkwardly*). Andddd got it.

BUCK. Don't Instagram that!

CLARISSA. Too late Buck, our photo's already cross-platform. I've got like seven thousand followers on Twitter.

BUCK. *How?*

CLARISSA. Evangelical Twitter's a thing. So lookout Eddie, here we come! (*Calling out.*) Clarissa for President! Vote Clarissa for senior class president! Oh, Song Dongjun! Take a pin. (*She exits.*)

BUCK. Oh what a very nice poster, lemme just – (*She drops it and rolls over it again and again.*) YEP. There we go. That oughta do it.

RICHARD. That's rather aggressive.

BUCK. I hate her! She's the *worst*.

RICHARD. And when someone's the worst we run 'em over.

BUCK. Pretty much.

RICHARD. Buck, lemme float this: what if we could knock Clarissa out of the running entirely?

BUCK. Why bother? Eddie's got this thing locked.

RICHARD. But what if he doesn't? What if Clarissa applies her irritating overachieving tendencies towards pestering the electorate out of their votes?

BUCK. Dude. That would suck.

RICHARD. So then how do we stop it? Here's something. Clarissa's an overachiever but she's not very smart. Her grades are just borderline.

BUCK. So?

RICHARD. So in order to run for election you have to hold at least a B average.

BUCK. Okay…

RICHARD. Okay so aren't you a teacher's assistant in at least half her classes? You're a TA for Ms York. That covers Class Council and English. And aren't you her Chemistry TA?

BUCK. Not exactly, I just have access to the grade books cuz I do data entry for the science department cuz of medically-excused PE. *Huh huh...* wouldn't it be, wouldn't it be funny if...

RICHARD *cocks his head.*

Nooooo, no I could never do that!

RICHARD. *No of course not.*

BUCK. Ooooh, you are *evil*!

RICHARD. No *you are*.

BUCK. But Ms York locks up her shit! It's not like I'd even have access –

RICHARD. Access, are you kidding? You're a total kleptomaniac Buck. Don't you remember, you're the one that taught me how to do *this*.

RICHARD *does a weird hand gesture thing and produces* BUCK*'s keys.*

BUCK. Hey my keys! Oh yeah I did teach you that. I gotta go...

RICHARD. Verily Buck. Hie thee hence.

BUCK. Thou HAST to stop talking like that. For real, fuckin' *stop*. (*She exits*.)

[handwritten annotations: Richard pretty vulnerable in this scene — still skeptical but vulnerable]

Scene Three – Dance Studio

The scenery shifts around RICHARD *as he speaks and now we're in a dance studio.* ANNE*'s stretching as* RICHARD *joins in.*

RICHARD. Pity poor Buck. She believes herself to be acting in Eddie's service yet serves only me.

And yet, for the moment, I'm not thinking about Buck, or the elections. I'm thinking about ballet barres, and mirrors. The wall-length mirrors where there's no place to hide the gracelessness with which I shamble about. I'm thinking of how there's the speech of our words and how my words can be made to dissemble, but then there's speech of our bodies, and in that I am stilted, deformed. I see the defects reflected again and again in these mirrors, and all of my words fall short. I am *thinking...* that Anne's dance clothes are a little bit see-through, and when she bends the right way I can just make out the shape of her...

ANNE. I like what I'm seeing!

RICHARD (*caught*). You what?! I, um, I wasn't looking! (*He turns away, ashamed.*)

ANNE. Sorry I just meant I like how you're stretching /

RICHARD (*relieved*). Ohhhh.

ANNE. / you have a great range of motion on the left, I can totally work with that.

RICHARD. Oh yeah, um. Okay.

ANNE. But unfortunately your right side's a little bit spazzy, which is gonna be harder to work with.

RICHARD. 'Spazzy.' Is that the technical term?

ANNE. I mean kind of.

RICHARD. That's fine. I can just *spaz hands*. (*He does jazz hands.*)

ANNE. That's right, *Spazzersize*!

RICHARD. You're listening to the Quiet Storm, for allllll of your smooooth spazz hits.

ANNE (*sings, à-la* Chicago). 'Come on babe why don't we paint the town. And all that Spaz!'

RICHARD. 'And all that Spaz!'

ANNE. 'I'm gonna knock my knees and flail my arm around. And all that Spaz!'

RICHARD. 'And all that Spaz!'

ANNE. Hey!

BOTH. 'All. That. Spaaaazzzzz.'

They laugh together, then lickety-split...

RICHARD. You know that's not funny, right, because I was born this way and I'm physically incapable of complete muscle control?

ANNE. Jesus, I was just joking around, I'm so sorry!

RICHARD (*laughs*). I just totally liberal-guilted you...

ANNE. Oh... Ohhh God. Don't do that to me!

RICHARD. So what did you wanna teach me?

ANNE. Oh, right. Well they'll probably be playing mostly hip hop at Sadie Hawkins so I guess I could show you a couple of those moves. I dunno just move around, let me see you.

He does nothing.

Five, six, seven, eight.

He does something half-assed.

C'mon dude, *commit* to it.

RICHARD. I am!

ANNE. This? (*Imitating his half-assed motion.*) This is what you're bringing to the dance floor? I wanna see your full-swag phone cranked up jumpin-on-the-bed and dabbing midnight-dance-party moves like nobody's watching.

RICHARD. Which is easy with all of these *mirrors*.

ANNE. DO IT.

RICHARD. Fine, what about this? (*He moves as best he can.*)

ANNE. *Good*. There ya go! Less arm movement. More in the hips.

He does pretty much the same thing.

Put the arm down! Relax.

She guides him.

Now sway. Gyrate a little.

RICHARD. You want me to *gyrate*. Or how about this, huh? (*He does something over the top.*) You want me to… you want me to… you want me to… (*He slips and falls.*) *Shit*.

ANNE. Whoa. Are you okay?

She goes over to help him but he pushes her off.

RICHARD. I got it, I'm fine. (*Pause*.) FUCK.

ANNE. That's not serious, right – you were messing around?

RICHARD. Actually, I fall down all the time.

ANNE. Seriously?

RICHARD. Yes seriously.

ANNE. Why, because of –

RICHARD. Because of my disability? Yeah *that*.

ANNE. Jeez I never knew.

RICHARD. Right well. You were busy. With being more popular than anyone else.

ANNE. You know I'm really *not* popular.

RICHARD. Whatever.

ANNE. I mean. People know I dated Eddie but it's not like anybody knows *me*.

RICHARD. Yeah it's hard at the top.

ANNE. What are you…

RICHARD. Nothing. Let's just keep going.

ANNE. Richard, can I ask? What's it like? Like the way that you move, what does it feel like to you? It's just I'm obsessed with movement, and the way that you move – there's this definite poetry to it. But it also looks painful. Does it hurt your joints, even? Moving that way? If that's too much to ask I'm sorry.

RICHARD. No, it's fine, I've actually never been asked. To be honest 'how it feels' is probably how you feel. My brain thinks that all of me's moving. Though my severed nerves and atrophied muscles might disagree. But to me my movement feels normal. 'Til someone reminds me I'm not.

ANNE. Shit. I'm sorry.

RICHARD. And it is painful. Moving this way. Joint pain from the torquing. Muscle pain from my left leg being so overworked. My right shoulder's pretty much permanently dislocated though I don't really feel that. And my right hip – the doctors say I need a replacement like ASAP, sorry does this even answer your question?

ANNE. Totally. *Thank you*. For, you know, just for –

RICHARD. I told you, it's fine. It's actually nice.

ANNE. Well I can't do anything for the pain but for your movement? I've got a ton of ideas. Dancing – at least this kind of fake-ass school-dance dancing – it's less about fast motion and just – (*She approaches*.) Can I?

RICHARD. Yes. You may touch me.

ANNE (*she adjusts his body and sets him in motion*). Here, just – like that, see? Slow. Slow but on the beat. Feel it in your body – there you go. Move.

RICHARD (*genuinely moved*). Whoa.

ANNE. And now I move with you. Good!

They're in motion together.

RICHARD. How often do you come here Anne?

ANNE. Every day right after school, plus every Saturday morning.

RICHARD. Six days a week?? Doing what?

ANNE. Workin' my butt off, that's what. I do hip hop, modern, a dash of ballet. I want to move to New York City once we graduate so I'll probably apply to Fordham, Juilliard, NYU.

Fordham pairs up with Alvin Ailey, which would be such an incredible dream. Keep doing what you're doing – check this.

She takes off around him, does a mini-performance.

RICHARD (*impressed*). Whaaaaat.

ANNE (*immediately apologetic*). I mean who knows what'll happen with auditions but I've gotta get out of here, right? Gotta get so good at dance that those jaded-ass New York City dance teachers can't deny me, can't ignore that I'm here.

RICHARD (*he's stopped to admire her*). I get that Anne.

ANNE. Wait, don't stop – you were doing so good.

RICHARD. Sorry, I was just – sorry. (*He starts up again.*) Wait, you don't like it at Roseland?

ANNE. Why would I? So cliquish. Everyone's always so up in each other's shit about who's sleeping with who or who got the invite to which parties and it's like, People: it's *high school*. This is not life or death.

RICHARD. But you and Eddie…

ANNE. What about me and Eddie?

RICHARD. You just seemed like you ran the whole school.

ANNE. Yeah well. People break up. As if I even *wanted* to…

RICHARD. What? Wanted to what?

ANNE. Just… fuck Eddie okay? When I get out of here on a dance scholarship I'll be waving from the top of the

Empire State Building and I won't think twice about
Roseland or Eddie or any of this shit.

RICHARD. Sure, and that plan would work. Were it not merely
our junior year.

ANNE. Well that's where you come in, right? Aren't you my
charm offensive?

RICHARD. Oh yes, I'm your good-luck charm. Or not even
a charm, more like a talisman. A harbinger of the order
to come.

ANNE. You're kind of a weirdo you know that?

RICHARD. *Yeah.*

ANNE. What about you? What are you gonna do when you get
out of Roseland?

RICHARD. I'd rather shake things up here than rely on some
kind of escape plan.

ANNE. What's that supposed to mean?

RICHARD (*he stops*). It means that if I were your boyfriend
I would've done everything I could to hold on to you here
and now.

ANNE. One sec. Richard I didn't think that you'd –

RICHARD. What? Make a move? On the hottest, most talented
girl in the school? Why? Because I'm disabled that means
I have to be some kind of asexual too? I'm here Anne.

ANNE. I know that you're here.

RICHARD. Then in all these reflections of you and me here,
can you see a vision where the risk of falling is worth the
reward of the dance?

ANNE (*she considers this*). *Okay.*

   They kiss. Lights out. In the darkness…

RICHARD. Did anyone else fucking SEE THAT?

Scene Four – Classroom

CLARISSA (*looking at a paper*). Reese's *Feces*. Ms York what are we doing here? I failed my grade check? (*Smiley.*) That's *not* possible.

ELIZABETH. It's imminently possible. It's actually fact.

CLARISSA (*fracturing*). But, but I'm a good student!

ELIZABETH. Oh, you're a great student. Or at least above average, let's go with that. But you can't run for president. The rules are the rules.

CLARISSA. Frick your rules. Frick your rules in the butt.

ELIZABETH (*to* RICHARD *et al*). GUYS. Go to lunch.

EDDIE. Yeah, I'm good.

BUCK. Just packin' my stuff…

RICHARD. My legs don't work good.

CLARISSA. Ms York you already accepted my candidate papers! Plus, *plus* my signature page. Gathering two hundred signatures was *not* trivial. It shows the people want me on their ballots!

ELIZABETH. Clarissa. I appreciate the *lunch period* you spent gathering signatures. But your GPA is not above board.

CLARISSA. How am I getting a B-minus in English? Or Class Council?! It's *Class frickin' Council*. Eddie's getting an A and he can't even add fractions!

EDDIE (*to* BUCK). What's fractions?

ELIZABETH. You three? Out!

CLARISSA. No, no, you stay! I don't futzin' care! I don't futzin' care who knows you're a *cheater*. I'm out of order?? You're out of order!

ELIZABETH. When did I say you're out of order?

CLARISSA. This whole classroom's out of order! (*Insta-cries, slaps herself, hushed self-admonishment.*) *Stoppit.*

ELIZABETH. Clarissa, I know it's upsetting but you're frequently tardy. Three tardies a term results in a mandatory grade drop.

CLARISSA. I haven't been tardy that much!

ELIZABETH. Yes you have. I note it every time in my book.

BUCK. That she do.

CLARISSA (*to* BUCK). Oh shut up. (*To* ELIZABETH.) What about the fact – the FACT! – that Richard is late all the time and you never penalize him?

ELIZABETH. This is your whole GPA, it's not just my class. Richard passed his grade check. Eddie passed his.

CLARISSA. Richard passed? Why are we doing grade checks on Richard?

ELIZABETH. Because they are running for president and you are not.

EDDIE. Yo, what?

BUCK. Seriously?

CLARISSA. I knew it! You frickin' liar.

ELIZABETH. Maybe you wouldn't be tardy if you weren't doing so many inter-period *prayer circles*.

RICHARD/BUCK/EDDIE. Uh-oh.

CLARISSA. I'm sorry?

ELIZABETH. What? Nothing.

CLARISSA. Are you questioning my *faith*? Is this some kind of Christian purge of the ballot?!

ELIZABETH. Okay, *no*. Clarissa, you pipe down this instant or I'm taking you to the Tower.

CLARISSA. The what?

ELIZABETH. You know, the Tower. The principal's office? It's shaped like a tower. Your behavior right now is abhorrent.

CLARISSA. You are the stupidest person in history. How'd you become a teacher? You couldn't teach a baby to shit!

ELIZABETH. That's it Clarissa, you go to The Tower.

CLARISSA. But but but senior class president! *Stanford.* Summers in Paris? Harvard MBA. *Lean In*? Google?! If I don't get president I just, *crap.* Aw poopin' crap. Just… crap.

ELIZABETH. Move it little miss.

CLARISSA *and* ELIZABETH *exit.*

BUCK/RICHARD. OHHHHHHH.

BUCK. She shouldn't be tardy so much. The Lord sees that you know.

RICHARD (*to* EDDIE). C'mon, admit it. That was awesome.

EDDIE. Yeah. We're not friends. We're not sharing a moment right now. I heard what Ms York said.

BUCK. Yeah, you *are too* running for president.

RICHARD. Fine, I'll admit it. *I want to be president!* Is that okay with you Buck?

BUCK. Run or don't run, I don't care, just don't be a weasel about it.

EDDIE. Well I fuckin care. Yo, you think you're running for *president*?! Well you can't run. *Legs.*

RICHARD. You nitwit you can't even deliver the joke. It's, 'How you gonna run for president when your legs don't work?'

EDDIE. I said what I said! You think you're so smart, Crooked Dick? Well you're not. I can throw a sixty-yard pass… to *myself.* So now who's got the cojones, huh retard?

BUCK. Richard don't engage.

RICHARD. Ohhhkkkay. You know the ironic thing, Eddie? People hate me just by looking at me when clearly you're the one they should hate because you're pure evil running on a simian brain.

BUCK. Richard.

RICHARD. It's just that at some point after seventeen years of being treated like an asshole, something just snaps in you. At some point you go, '*Fine. You want me to be evil, then let me be evil.* You think I'm scary-looking, then good. Be afraid.' It's like what's inside us no longer matters. Our surfaces smother our guts.

EDDIE. . . . Did you just call me an asshole?

RICHARD. *What?*

EDDIE. I heard the word asshole.

RICHARD. Yeah but in the context of...

EDDIE. I'ma stick my *dick* up your context. (*He grabs* RICHARD.) You think you can step on my turf and I won't hunt you down? Drop out of the race.

He gives RICHARD *a monster wedgie.*

RICHARD. Ahhhh. Nooooo. Noooooo!

EDDIE. Yo *fuck* are you wearing a *diaper*??

RICHARD. Fuck you!

EDDIE. That is so *Fucked Up*. Here's some advice big baby: Do not. (*Pull!*)

RICHARD. Ahh watch the balls –

EDDIE. Fuck with me. (*Pull!*)

RICHARD. My *balls* you dumb fuck!

EDDIE. Got it?

He drops RICHARD *to the floor.*

BUCK. This was avoidable!

EDDIE. This... this was good. This was like a – whaddya call it – like a real live presidential debate. Later Limp Dick. (*To* BUCK.) Milady. (*Yelling.*) *Stallion Pride! Whaat whaa?* (*He exits.*)

RICHARD. Motherfucker! Piece of motherfucking – I will murder your *children*. (*To* BUCK.) You still think he's *nice*?

BUCK. No, you know what? I'm not sorry he did that. You said taking out Clarissa was for his benefit.

RICHARD. It was for all of us.

BUCK. Well I don't appreciate being used.

RICHARD. I mean what do you want me to say here Buck?

BUCK. I dunno, 'Sorry for using you?'

RICHARD. Sorry.

BUCK. Richard, why didn't you just say you were running? You can be honest with me, we're friends.

RICHARD. Oh yeah then prove it. Be a pal and lower Eddie's grades for me.

BUCK. I'm not gonna do that. Richard why would I do that?

RICHARD. Uh-huh such a good *friend*. You already have blood on your hands. Why stop at Clarissa? Why not ride this elevator all the way to the top?

BUCK. Because I'm fine where I am. I don't have a big gaping hole in my soul that yearns to be filled with absolute power, ya sinister horcrux. Richard, if someone pulled on my underwear to the point that it ruptured my taint, I think I might call a time-out.

RICHARD. Yeah well that's you.

BUCK. Richard. Why can't you be happy just being yourself?

RICHARD. Myself. Yeah, no thanks. Are you happy being yourself Buck? I hope so for your sake because you do know that this is as good as it gets for us. As shitty as Roseland is, it's Edenic compared to the real world. You think anyone's gonna give a *shit* about us, out there, once our bodies start turning against us more and more every day? This isn't our awkward phase, it's the rest of our lives.

BUCK. Yes Batman, you're so very brooding. Tell me more about the time your mom and dad took you to see the opera.

RICHARD. I'm serious Buck. This election's our last chance at fixing the order of things. My victory enures to you because you and me are the same. And we're owed this!

BUCK. Umm. We aren't the same. You're the one who thinks you're owed something, not me. No one owes anyone shit. Richard your disability does not grant you license to act like a dick.

RICHARD. *Eddie's* the one who's a dick! God's bread, does no one else see this?! *Eddie*, that dumb ogre meathead. *Eddie* who is incapable of feeling. Incapable of nasal respiration. Incapable of reading without sounding out the words...

BUCK. Richard I *like* Eddie.

RICHARD. Wait. You like him as in you *like-like* him?

BUCK. *I dunno.* Shut up! Everybody shut up.

RICHARD. Ewwwww noooo. You actually think that *you'd* have a chance?

BUCK. Screw you. Why do you have a chance with Anne Margaret but I don't have one with Eddie?

RICHARD. Look at you and look at him.

BUCK. Why don't you look at *yourself*, Judgy von Judgerstein, you ain't no first-prize pig. Eddie couldn't even handle all this. I'm down to clown! I will rock that boy's world!

RICHARD. How would that even *work*?

BUCK. Fuck you Turd Town! Quit being an ableist fuck.

RICHARD. I can't be 'ableist', I'm disabled.

BUCK. Yeah, way to internalize that self-loathing, wouldn't wanna give it a sunburn. Listen I think I'm done helping you. From now on consider us frenemies. Neutral at best.

RICHARD. So you DEFY ME. A betrayer art thou? A tergiversator you?

BUCK. I don't know what that word is but that's the last word of French I wanna hear outta your French whore mouth.

RICHARD. *Buck*. Buddy! C'mooooonnnn.

BUCK. I'm not saying you're cancelled but you are removed from my Netflix queue. (*Calling off.*) Good luck with that taint. (*She exits.*)

RICHARD. Great. Without my grade-changing minion I'm screwed. Who can help me destroy Eddie. Who??

ANNE. Hey, you're late for our dance lesson, you forget about me?

RICHARD. Anne Margaret.

ANNE. That's rather formal. *Richard Gloucester*. Richard the Unpunctual. Hail Richard the – slightly disheveled, are you okay?

RICHARD. Look, could you just… lay off me? Maybe? I'm having a really bad day.

ANNE. I had a bad day too, you wanna do something about it?

Scene Five – Anne's Bedroom

ANNE *takes a hand to* RICHARD*'s cheek and kisses him.*
RICHARD *steps forward and the scene shifts around him.*

RICHARD. Wait. Is this happening? Is what I think's happening actually happening?! Whether sparked by my piteous state or by pheromones, Anne is taking me to her bedchambers. Ye Gods! O rapture! O culmination of all my fantastical yearnings! O… bollocks. I never thought I'd make it this far. How do – how do I even… uh-oh.

Lights shift in-scene as ANNE *approaches him.*

(*Uncomfortable, maybe even kind of batting her off.*) Uhh hey. Heyyy youuuu. I'm just gonna warn you this is gonna be *weeiiirrd*.

ANNE. Don't be so nervous.

RICHARD. Ahhhh but it is though. It's extremely *weird* down there. I'm not even sure what-all works.

ANNE. Shall we have a look and find out?

RICHARD. Yeah okay but just to be – just, full disclosure? I'm wearing a diaper. You were going to find out anyway so there it is Anne. I'm an adult diaper wearer. Does that repulse you, that I'm a big baby, or is that your kink? I'm pretty sure that's nobody's kink. I should leave.

ANNE. Hey nobody asked for that. Richard? Calm the fuck *down*.

RICHARD. Oh my *God* I am just. I've got diarrhea of the mouth don't I, the diaper should be on my face.

ANNE. Let's just. Enter this. With no preconceptions.

RICHARD. Why? I've got preconceptions about you, I'm hoping you'll knock my socks off.

ANNE. Oh ha ha it's a good thing you're such a good kisser then.

RICHARD. Yeah no *obviously*, I'm obviously that. I am?

ANNE. Quit being thirsty for likes. And you're not the only one with baggage so let's take it slow. Hell I *wanna* take it slow.

RICHARD. Yeah?

ANNE. Yeah.

They kiss. They do more stuff.

Actually –

RICHARD. Oh God I knew it, I fuckin *Knew* it.

ANNE. No no, it's not you.

RICHARD. No of course not.

ANNE. Richard I have been down this road, getting physical super-early, and I thought I was ready but maybe I'm not.

RICHARD. Well if it's me we're talking about I'm quite sure you'll never be ready.

ANNE. I mean I don't know about never. We just started seeing each other!

RICHARD. I – Huh. So we're seeing each other.

ANNE. Yeah, so?

RICHARD. No it's just. I've never. I didn't know we were seeing each other. Like officially.

ANNE. Be… cause it isn't official.

RICHARD. No I know that. It's just that I've never had a girlfriend before.

ANNE. And you still don't. We're not boyfriend and girlfriend, we're just seeing each other.

RICHARD. I, um. Okay.

ANNE. Sorry, I know, like, I'm the one who asked you here. But I think what I really need is to concentrate on my dance and my grades and my future. And not get stuck –

RICHARD. With someone like me?

ANNE. It has nothing to do with you. Like I said there's your baggage and mine.

RICHARD. Anne, how did it end with Eddie?

ANNE. None of your business.

RICHARD. Did he try to pressure you into having sex and you wouldn't do it so he dumped you, is that it?

ANNE. Yeah I'm really not that much of a saint.

RICHARD. I see, was he violent then? Did Eddie physically abuse you Anne?

ANNE. Hey can you quit prying?

RICHARD. That's fine I just thought we were seeing each other. You say you're not ready for physical intimacy. What of verbal intimacy? Is it not mete that a lover be spared the sprynges of previous lovers, lest new lovers fall ensnared to the selfsame traps?

ANNE. Don't use the word 'lovers'.

RICHARD. Don't evade.

ANNE. Look I want to tell you but. No you know what? Forget it. You don't even know me.

RICHARD. No I do know you Anne. You and I are the only ones who see this school as it is – the glorification of masks and veneers? I'm the only person who looks past the surfaces and sees through to the real you.

ANNE. And I want to believe that but –

RICHARD. Jesus, what happened that's got you so guarded, so pained. What, you get pregnant or something? (*Grave pause.*) Oh shit. Oh shit Anne you did.

ANNE. Okay look. When Eddie and I were dating, it got physical really really fast. During football my parents would let me go to the games and then after the games we'd get in his truck and. And then yes, okay? Yes. I got pregnant. I'm such an *idiot*, it's such a stupid fucking cliché. We'd only not used protection once, but I guess that's just me, I'm just lucky.

RICHARD. And you're *still*, *now* –

ANNE. No… No, I thought about keeping it. Thought about telling my parents. But all of my plans? I'm not ready to be a *mother*. So after Christmas when my parents were away on a ski trip I went to an outpatient clinic. Alone. And that was pretty much that.

RICHARD. And Eddie dumped you when he found out? What a dick.

ANNE. No I dumped him. I never even told him. I couldn't.

RICHARD. I see.

ANNE. Richard, I really like you okay? Whatever this is – whatever thing we have going? You're definitely not at all what I was expecting and I'm sorry it's taken me so long to actually see you. But beyond that I have no clue where this is going, because I'm not looking for any more drama. God *why* did I have to – I shouldn't have even said anything. What's *wrong* with you Anne?

RICHARD. Hey. Hey, come here. (*He holds her.*) Thank you for being honest with me.

actually genuine or pretending?

this whole scene is him prying things out of her

Scene Six – Assembly

ANNE*'s bedroom fades and* RICHARD *steps forward.*

RICHARD. More like thank you for *nothing*. Oh God, Anne, don't tempt me. Don't vouchsafe your confidence with me, confess mine enemy's deepest secret, and expect me to *what*? Keep my mouth shut and *be decent*? What an indecent notion. Fut that.

And yet by striking down Eddie, there Anne's heart is felled too, and this doubled calamity must give us pause. What if decency is a viable choice? You guys: I'm dating Anne Margaret! Well, not dating, *sorta seeing*. But sorta seeing is something! What if all of it's possible? What if I challenge Eddie head-on, no dirty tricks, and we fight in the open as men. If Anne's heart is virtue let Richard's be virtuous too.

Very well. I'll run from temptation. I'll run Eddie through by running a clean campaign.

The stage gets set for a school assembly. ELIZABETH *enters.*

ELIZABETH. Settle down everybody. Settle down. NO YELLING! Thank you all for attending this mandatory assembly. I'm *very excited* to introduce our two presidential candidates. Eddie. And *Richard – yay*! Let's listen to them debate the issues and lay out their vision for the upcoming year. As I moderate the debate, you may join the democratic process by asking your town-hall-type questions either at the microphones or by livetweeting. Hashtag-Roseland-HS-Debate. Richard, let's start with you. Why do you want to be president?

RICHARD. Thank you Ms York. Roseland now stands on the precipice of a truly momentous decision. Do we accept this place as it is or dare we envision a rosier hue? Do we accede to the status quo or do we *re-seed* Roseland so that it blossoming blooms?

VOICE-OVER. Nerrrrrrd!

ELIZABETH. I see you Amanda!

RICHARD. Ahhh you see, this is my point exactly. There's a growing incivility to this school and I will end all the bullying. I'll stick up for you!

VOICE-OVER. Stick up your dick!

ELIZABETH. Amanda! You go to the Tower.

RICHARD (*over booing*). See, this is why when I'm elected I will ensure Roseland remains a safe space via a robust anti-harassment policy. I will protect marginalized groups. By electing me president you will prove to yourselves that we are above belittling each other over our outward differences.

ELIZABETH. *Wow*. Wow you guys! Eddie, my first question for you is now that you've been junior class president, what would you do differently next year, based on what you've learned?

EDDIE. Ummmm. Pretty much *Nothing*.

ELIZABETH. Excuse me? Let me rephrase.

EDDIE. No I get what you're saying. You saying I didn't do a good job or something.

ELIZABETH. Now I never said *that*.

EDDIE. Naw, you did, but here's the deal Ms York. I'd do nothing different because Roseland is the finest school in the country. The world even. This is already the best high school in history and this is *our time*, Stallions! Lemme hear that Stallion pride!

VOICE-OVER. Stallion pride! Stallion pride! Stallion pride!

ELIZABETH. GUYS. This is not a pep rally.

Projection:
@PattyMartinez: Q for @EddieQB. With your athletic commitments do you have the time, temperament, and the inclination to be senior class president?
#RoselandHSDebate

Ah. I see we have a livetweeted question from honors student Patty Martinez. '@EddieQB. With your athletic commitments do you have the time, temperament, and the inclination to be senior class president?'

EDDIE. Yep.

ELIZABETH. Okay, tersely put. Another question for Richard: what skills will you bring to the job?

RICHARD. Judgment. Discernment. A sense of morality that's adaptive yet rigid.

VOICE-OVER. *Rigid Dick!*

General laughter.

ELIZABETH. Quit that, Marcus, I see you!

EDDIE. Heh heh – rigid dick… Marcus you're my VP.

ELIZABETH. Actually he's not. The vice-president WILL be decided in a separate election and not by presidential fiat. Last time I checked we are still a democracy.

Projection:
@marcuspinkerton: Rigid Dick! #RoselandHSDebate

Marcus, you go to the Tower.

EDDIE. You're my *VP*!

ELIZABETH. He's not even running! Eddie, next question. As president you'd be in charge of ratifying the student-union fund.

EDDIE. Oh for real?

ELIZABETH. *Yes* I'm surprised you don't know that. Now do you think it's *fair* that the football team has requested the entirety of that fund for new bleachers?

EDDIE. Uh *yeah*. The school makes serious *bank* off of football.

ELIZABETH. What about the drama club? Is it fair for them to self-finance their costumes and sets?

EDDIE. I mean probably. Pretty much no one sees the school play.

ELIZABETH. Not true. We have a sold-out run *every year*.

EDDIE. Hey aren't you supposed to be impartial?

ELIZABETH. Well there is such a thing as *facts*.

EDDIE. Okay but I just feel like if you're the moderator and you're gonna throw shade all day am I sposed to take this serious, or –

ELIZABETH. Well I should hope so. This is a serious job. (*Off tweet sound of below.*) Oh, a tweeter!

Projection:
@amandarodriguez: kicked out of #RoselandHSDebate just for participating this is total bs

Okay ignore that.

@marcuspinkerton: Reply to @amandarodriguez OMG MEEE TOOOO

That too.

Projection:
@amandarodriguez: RT @marcuspinkerton Rigid Dick! #RoselandHSDebate

Oh, for the love of… Twitter is not the place for sarcasm and foolishness! (*Sees* EDDIE *tweeting.*) Eddie please put away your phone for the remainder of the debate.

Projection:
@EddieQB: @amandarodriguez @marcuspinkerton master debaters #RoselandHSDebate

(*Grimaces.*) Does anyone else have a question?

CLARISSA. I have a question Ms York.

ELIZABETH. Clarissa, thank goodness.

CLARISSA. As all of you know. I was brutally and probably illegally removed from the election.

ELIZABETH. CLARISSA. No.

CLARISSA. Excuse me, I haven't even gotten to my question.

Projection:
@ JefftheFlesh: Go home @ClarissaWWJD:
#RoselandHSDebate
@StallionFootball: @ClarissaWWJD Girrrrrl nobody likes
you #RoselandHSDebate
@JefftheFlesh: Jesus can't save @ClarissaWWJD from body
odor #RoselandHSDebate
@TonyVanGundy: Reply to @JefftheFlesh
@ClarissaWWJD, point to where the angel touched you.
Was it the bathing suit area?

ELIZABETH (*as the tweets roll in*). Hey! Hey hey hey. This is
    not a civil way of engaging with Clarissa's beliefs.

CLARISSA. Ms York I haven't even asked my question!

ELIZABETH. Clarissa I am begging you: read the room.

CLARISSA. My question is this: in the absence of my
    candidacy there is a real moral vacuum here on this stage.
    The presidency should be a position of moral leadership. So
    isn't it morally wrong we're being forced to choose between
    two non-believers? I think we should hold a referendum on
    changing the election's GPA requirements. Clarissa for
    reinstatement!

EDDIE. Yo are you for real? Does anyone care about this weird
    Bible thumpery?

Laughter.

CLARISSA. I represent a real constituency at this school. Mock
    me all you want Eddie but you WILL BURRRRRN.

EDDIE. Clarissa will you marry me?

ELIZABETH. Okaaay. Clarissa, why don't you go have a seat.

EDDIE. You have so much to teach me.

RICHARD. Clarissa I'd like to address your objection. I may
    not be a believer but I certainly share in your struggle.
    You're being persecuted. I've been persecuted my whole life.
    But together we all can transcend this. Isn't it John 5:11 that

says, 'Blessed are you when men revile you, and persecute you, and say all kinds of evil against you, for your reward in heaven is great.'

CLARISSA. That's Matthew 5:11.

RICHARD. Exactly.

EDDIE. Whaddya mean 'exactly'? You didn't even get the right dude.

RICHARD. It's so easy these days to take potshots at people for having religious beliefs, but I'm inspired by people who hold their convictions. Which is why I'll stick up for you and all of your brethren. Clarissa be my campaign manager.

CLARISSA. Social Media Manager. Stanford wants STEM skills.

RICHARD. Deal.

EDDIE. Can we get on with this? Clarissa, your campaign got benched so why don't you take a knee. You like that, that's a simile.

ELIZABETH. *Metaphor*. It's fine.

EDDIE (*to* RICHARD). As for *you* I don't know what game you're playing but everyone knows you don't belong on this stage. And I think deep down you know it too. You wanna change Roseland? Roseland doesn't *want* to change. (*Pause*.) Am I right Roseland?? Let's go Stallions. (*Clap clap clap clap clap*.)

VOICE-OVER (*crowd joining in*). Let's go Stallions. (*Clap clap clap clap clap*.)
Let's go Stallions. (*Clap clap clap clap clap*.)

ELIZABETH. No. Nooooo.
Guyyyys.

VOICE-OVER (*single leftover*). Let's go... aww.

ELIZABETH. We've gone off-track. Let's get back to the issues.

RICHARD. Yeah, here's the issue. Eddie: you are dangerously unqualified for this job.

EDDIE. Actually? I've been doing this job all year.

RICHARD. You have been *murdering* this job. You haven't served this school an iota, you vainglorious coxcomb – you and your empty bravado. This school devolves daily beneath your blusterous malfeasance yet all you do is gad about in the parking lot.

EDDIE. I leave everything on the field.

RICHARD. Including any actual work? You are a lamprey that feeds off your own braggadocio, and no one is willing to tell you the truth of the matter but me.

EDDIE. Ms York?

RICHARD. I will accede to your smug demagoguery no longer, you self-serving tyrant. What know ye of governance, monster. What knowst thou of the law?

EDDIE. Screw *you*, man. My stepdad's a *lawyer*.

RICHARD. And your birth father abandoned you as a child and you've been trying to touchdown the hurt away ever since.

VOICE-OVER (*crowd*). OHHHHHH!

ELIZABETH (*guffaws despite herself, then*). Terrible. That's terrible…

EDDIE. Whatever *freak*, you think anyone at Roseland wants to be led by a total social outcast.

RICHARD. UM would a total social outcast be dating Anne Margaret?

General-intrigue grumbles.

EDDIE. Dude what?

RICHARD. Ohhh that's right Eddie. I stole your girlfriend.

EDDIE. Bull SHIT you're dating Anne.

ELIZABETH. *Guys!*

EDDIE. You are not dating Anne you crip FREAK.

ELIZABETH. HEY.

RICHARD. I AM dating Anne and I'll prove it. Stand up Anne.

Lights up on ANNE. *Deer in the headlights.*

Anne say something. (*Pause.*) Go.

ANNE *bolts.*

EDDIE. Ahhh haaa haaa haaaa. Ya told her to go.

RICHARD. Goddammit, Anne!

ELIZABETH. Okay I've had enough. This is not the elevated
discourse a democracy should be and I'm ashamed of all of
you. This assembly is over. Dismissed.

General hubbub as crowd dissipates.

(*To run crew.*) Oh yeah let's livetweet the debate. Great idea
Janice.

(*To* EDDIE/RICHARD.) What is wrong with you two?!

(*To* RICHARD.) Using this debate as a forum to brag about
girlfriends?!

RICHARD. What else can I do?? If all that matters is his
personality cult what tactics are left? I had real ideas Ms York!

ELIZABETH. But we cannot allow ourselves to sink to his
level. Next time try *keeping* your head. (*She exits.*)

EDDIE. Some stunt Mr Pretzels.

RICHARD. Don't call me that!

EDDIE. Nice try with the Anne thing. Sad.

RICHARD. And yet I am dating Anne.

EDDIE. She just jilted you in front of the entire school, man!
Wake up. Are you really that lonely? If you're lonely, go stop
by 4H Club. They'll hook you up with a hot-looking goat.

RICHARD. I don't need to date a goat anymore you cretinous
mesomorph.

EDDIE. AnyMORE?

RICHARD. Eddie I prithee do not *fuck* with me today. Fie on it Eddie. Dyou really want proof? Cuz I could proffer all the proof that you need.

EDDIE. The fuck is that sposed to mean?

RICHARD. Do you ever wonder whyyyy Anne dumped you. I know why. But I'll never tell.

EDDIE. There's nothing to tell. Because anyway, I, I'm, like, the one that dumped her.

RICHARD. Ohhh Eddie. Your position's so *fragile* right now. And look how you *know* it. The fear in your saucer eyes, I could drink it up like a cat.

EDDIE. That's great. Listen, I've got spring training right now? I'm very busy preparing my body for what will obviously become my professional career, given that that is what happens for most high-school athletes. But let's be clear: You will never be president. You are not dating Anne. And you never will. Richard, what you are is a cripple, and hot girls don't go for cripples, because even pity has limits. You are not dating Anne because you're not only a cripple you're also a malicious unlikeable troll, and for these reasons you will be lonely for the rest of your miserable, short, unremarkable life. See you at the ballot box BITCH. (*He exits.*)

RICHARD. God *damn* it!

Scene Seven – Dance Studio

RICHARD. Hey. The door was locked –

ANNE. *Yeah* so maybe you should recognize where you're unwanted.

RICHARD. Right so instead of that I got the front-desk guy to give me the key. Or rather I purloined it. Ka-Pow! (*He flashes the key.*) Thanks for all your support back there.

ANNE. Are you for real? How frickin' DARE you call me out like that? In front of the whole fucking school?

RICHARD. Well are we seeing each other or not?!

ANNE. DUDE I'm not your *campaign wife*. I never signed up for that.

RICHARD. Oh I seeeee Anne, of course. When it's us in private that's fine. But once I ask you to heave your heart into your mouth *just a little*? That's when you show me the door.

ANNE. Richard there is a WORLD of difference between not being public with you versus letting you march me out at *assembly*. Do you not get the difference?

RICHARD. You're ashamed of me!

ANNE. Nice try but that's really not it.

RICHARD. No, of course you are. You've every right to be. Look at me and look at you.

ANNE. Hey you don't get to play victim, you are not the wronged party here.

RICHARD.…Fine Anne. I apologize for my conduct, which was unseemly. Eddie provoked me, I reacted inexcusably, and for that I'm at fault.

ANNE. *Yeah*.

RICHARD. But then where do we go from here? If you're too ashamed to be with me there's literally no place to go. What do we do at the dance? Hide in the broom closet? Put paper bags on our heads?

ANNE. I'm not sure there's gonna be a dance anymore.

RICHARD. When you were with Eddie you weren't this mousy hideabout person. I wonder what changed.

ANNE. Richard you know what changed!

RICHARD. I just – I don't understand. This self-imposed exile over one simple mistake? So what if you had an abortion? It's honestly not a big deal.

ANNE. It's a huge fucking deal for *me* OKAY?

RICHARD. No – not that it's not a big deal, but –

ANNE. Seriously. All I have to do is survive here for another year and a half.

RICHARD. 'Survive.' What kind of mentality is 'survive'?

ANNE. I'm not – I don't know who you think I am: a bauble, a trophy, someone who's immune to the snickers of gossiping mean girls. Whatever you think I am, I am not that, okay?

RICHARD. But the confident girl I see in this room.

ANNE. This room is where I go to escape! Why do you think I'm here six days a week? I just have to stay under the radar long enough to get the fuck out of town and go be a whole new person once I finally get to New York.

RICHARD. Funny, I love the person who's standing before me right now.

ANNE. Oh really? You love someone too stupid to use protection. You love someone *who hates herself.*

RICHARD. You don't hate yourself, Anne.

ANNE. I hate the idiot who could throw away her whole future like that.

RICHARD. Okay. And I get that, but…

ANNE. Honestly you *don't.* You have no idea what I went through. All these nurses barging in and out of the room but none of them held my hand. They looked at their clipboards more than they looked at me. And it's like – I'm a dancer,

I've been dancing my whole life, but to them I'm nothing more than an idiot teen. And they're right. I am that. So why should they think any more of me than I am? I was. I was completely alone for it. I bled for four days and had no one but the internet to tell me if it was normal or not.

RICHARD. I wish I'd been there for you. Eddie should've been there for sure. But he was too busy thinking of nobody else but himself.

ANNE. This isn't about Eddie.

RICHARD. Of course it is, or was he not *involved*? He gets to go on blissfully unaware of his actions while you bear the burden alone. Why do you keep protecting him?

ANNE. I'm not protecting him, I'm protecting myself!

RICHARD. Eddie's an absolute irresponsible bastard. Do you not *get that*?

ANNE. You know what, do me a favor and never mention Eddie again. It's *ugly*, okay? It's a side of you I don't care to see.

RICHARD. You still have feelings for him.

ANNE. Richard what'd I just say?

RICHARD. If you never got pregnant, would you be with him still? Would we be standing here now? Of course not.

ANNE. But we are here now.

RICHARD. Do you still love him?

ANNE. RICHARD.

RICHARD. Do you? Yes or no?

ANNE. I don't know! I don't fuckin' *have* to know! Richard we are in *high school*. I mean what does love mean? It's not even real.

RICHARD. It's real to me. What of what we have now? Is *this* not real? If it's not real what is it? A rebound? A joke? A pity date gone clownishly long? Certainly this isn't something you're proud of outside these four walls, so I guess we've found the limits of pity, the confines of charitable deeds.

ANNE. Richard I've told you things no one else on this earth knows about me but you. I've spent more time with you – opened myself up to you more than with anyone. And you still need me to tell you what this is?

RICHARD. What does it matter what this is, if all that this is gets sepulchered in this room.

ANNE. Fine, you want me to prove I'm not ashamed to be in public with you, then you prove you're not the nasty resentful person I saw at assembly today. This jealousy towards Eddie? The way that you *fixate*? And the election is only making it worse. So you know what? I'll go to the dance with you. But you have to drop out of the race. I mean fuck Eddie right? You're with me now.

RICHARD. Not if this isn't real.

ANNE. I'm saying: in whatever weird contest you have in your head, haven't you already won?

ANNE *fades away*. RICHARD *steps forward*.

RICHARD. Eddie's hide. Or Anne's love. Which is the real prize?

Is it the flower of love that unfurls before me or is it the spoils of war, the fruits of the victory garden. O accursed Demeter! You've salted the earth, the soil is soiled. Now does the seed of doubt grow in me, its briars rending my insides through.

Suppose I drop the election. Let Eddie get what he wants, like he always does. I try to take solace in Anne's love but Anne's love isn't real, she just said so. Man's love is fickle and that's why it's best to be feared. Flash-forward a month and Anne tires of me. Flash-forward a year and she'll laugh at the very memory of holding this gnarled body to hers. Two years from now and Anne's a whole different person and even the memory of me will be gone. These brief moments of happiness: that's all that one such as me ever gets. I am Buck, running in a touchdown that doesn't count, for a crowd that cheers out of pity and fear.

Hush you now these tremulous notions. Steel thy resolve and silence thy mewling incertitude. Eddie's hide or Anne's love. I look deep inside and grab for the one prize that's real.

Lights shift.

Scene Eight – School Dance

Music plays. School-dance lighting, yay! RICHARD *quick-changes offstage.*

ANNE. Richard, you ready? What's wrong? Are you nervous? Jesus if anything I'm the one who should be nervous. I'm going out with the disabled guy! Not that I see you that way. It's just – this is kind of my first time out in public since football season. Lot of… lot of eyes watching. Not that I'm not happy to be here with you. But not if you're nervous about it. Because I'm not nervous, are YOU? (*Pause.*) Richard, seriously, what the fuck? Going to the dance was your dumb idea, and all you can do is cower in the hallway?

RICHARD (*enters in a white tux*). I'm not cowering. I just want to take it all in. You. The music. The lights. I want to remember this moment exactly, the moment when my future opened before me and for once it was not so immutable.

ANNE. I mean… I don't know about all of that. It's a lame fuckin' dance in the gym.

RICHARD. It's more than that Anne. This is my cotillion ball, if you will.

ANNE. That's a basketball hoop, if you will. I can't believe they call this a *dance floor*. If my movement coach saw me dancing on this she would freak.

VOICE-OVER (*DJ*). All right DJ Beats-upon-Avon on the wheels of steel. Roseland High School Sadie Hawkins Dance – where the *lady* decides. Here's one lady's special request song. *Awwww yeaaah…*

ANNE. C'mon c'mon c'mon! We got this.

Music thumps up in earnest. ANNE *and* RICHARD *do an adorable dance routine. It's FABULOUS. If it's not fabulous enough, you spent too much time doing table work. Then a slow song kicks in. They hold each other.*

Omigod that was great!

RICHARD. I was just trying to keep up with you!

ANNE. We crusht that shyaaat.

RICHARD. They better not play anymore fast songs cuz that's all the moves that I've got.

ELIZABETH *enters.*

ELIZABETH. Oh kids that was *wonderful*! Richard I had no idea you could dance!

RICHARD. She's the one who taught me!

ELIZABETH. You taught him all THAT? What a beautiful gift you've been given. You're a good person.

ANNE....Thanks.

ELIZABETH (*looking off*). Oh hell no Song Dongjun! Is that a *flask*? Song Dongjun you back *away* from the punch bowl this instant! That is IT. Your ass OUTSIDE, with me. We are going to the Tower. (*To* RICHARD.) Excuse me. (*She exits.*)

ANNE. Hey: I'm really proud of you.

RICHARD. Yeah, why? Because our *PR stunt* is working?

ANNE. No, I'm proud that you worked really hard for something, and that all of your efforts paid off.

RICHARD. And it looks good for you socially, too, like you're doing your charity work.

ANNE. Stop turning this dance into some kind of transactional commerce thing. I mean, sure, maybe that's how it started. But I do want to be here with you.

RICHARD. So – what – you're saying this is a date?

ANNE. Shocking right.

RICHARD (*guilty*). No but it's not a *real date*. I mean maybe I tricked you. Maybe this is a transaction because all relationships are transactional. Or maybe. Anne, maybe I'm not who you think I am.

ANNE. Or maybe just have fun at this dance and stop wigging out. Look, I know you're not perfect. I know you can be semi-shady. But you didn't have to trick me, I'm here. Thank you for letting the election go.

RICHARD. Y-yeah.

ANNE. I know that was hard for you.

RICHARD. Of course.

ANNE. And I'm sorry I've been so afraid to be out in public. It was never a reflection on you, it was... well you know what it was. But please just don't ever feel like I'm embarrassed of you. Okay Richard? Like just be yourself.

RICHARD. Myself. Anne I think I made a mistake. Can we go somewhere where we can talk?

BUCK *enters*.

BUCK. Anne! Richard! Thank God I found you. Listen, I don't know if this is some kind of sick joke or what. But Anne, you need to look at your Twitter feed right fucking now.

ANNE. My Twitter feed? What're you talking about? (*She takes out her phone*.) Oh... Oh my God! Oh my *God*!

We hear voice-overs of various Tweets cutting into the dance music, starting with CLARISSA's fake account. These are projected over the dance lighting and over the actors' bodies. We are now in a theatricalized social-media shit storm.

VOICE-OVER (@RHSGOSSIPGIRL). Hey @RoselandHS did you know @EddieQB got a girl pregnant? #NotMyPresident #StallionShame

VOICE-OVER (CLARISSA). Whoa, @RHSGossipGirl @EddieQB did WHAT?

VOICE-OVER (*Clarissa fake account*). @EddieQB forced this girl to get an abortion

VOICE-OVER (CLARISSA). Hey @RoselandHS did you know @EddieQB is a #childmurderer #StallionShame

VOICE-OVER. Despicable @EddieQB

VOICE-OVER. @RoselandHS Always use protection #StallionShame

VOICE-OVER. Wait was this with @annemargaret? This has to be @annemargaret

ANNE. Oh my God. Oh my God. What the FUCK!

VOICE-OVER. Yo did u see this?? @annemargaret totally got an abortion!

VOICE-OVER. RT @annemargaret – Dude what a slut

VOICE-OVER. @annemargaret @EddieQB Is this for real? #whaaaat?

VOICE-OVER. @annemargaret I ammm the ghooost of #annesdeadbaby

VOICE-OVER. @annemargaret Kill yourself

VOICE-OVER. @annemargaret God sees all. So does Twitter

VOICE-OVER. Ew, you guys look: Anne had an abortion!

VOICE-OVER. Retweeting

VOICE-OVER. Retweet

VOICE-OVER. #annesdeadbaby – so sad

ANNE. I… I can't even… Richard?

RICHARD. It was only supposed to be about him.

    EDDIE *enters, with* CLARISSA *following.*

EDDIE. Is it true Anne?

ANNE *stares at the floor*.

ANNE (*whispered*). No, no, no, no...

EDDIE. You were pregnant? How could you not tell me?

ANNE (*whispered*). No, no, no, no...

RICHARD. I said target Eddie, not her.

CLARISSA. You knew what this was.

EDDIE. Do you know how fucked up this is? To find this out on my phone? I knew you wouldn't just dump me for no reason. Anne, *look at me*. (*He shakes her.*)

RICHARD. Hey you don't fucking *touch* her.

EDDIE. Stay out of this Cripple Dick.

RICHARD. Make me.

EDDIE. I said stay out of this.

BUCK. Look maybe we should all just back off. Anne, are you okay?

ANNE *looks up, ashen. Everyone stares at her. Silence*.

ANNE. I... I just... I can't do this anymore. I can't... (*She darts off.*)

RICHARD. Anne, wait!

EDDIE. This is bullshit. (*He starts to exit.*)

RICHARD. Eddie, stop right there villain.

EDDIE. Yo you do not wanna FUCK with me now. You think this is funny?

RICHARD. You tell me. You're the one who forced her into having an abortion then *left her*. Explain yourself Eddie. Explain yourself to everyone here.

EDDIE. I don't have to explain. I *love* her, okay? I. Love. Her.

RICHARD. But you didn't love her enough. I will stick by her like you never could. (*To the crowd.*) This is the man that he is. This is he!

EDDIE *runs off in pursuit of* ANNE.

ELIZABETH (*enters*). What the HELL's going on here? What the hell crazy SHIT are you guys saying on Twitter. Uh-uh, you idiots, we are on lockdown 'til we find out who started this.

RICHARD (*indicating* CLARISSA). Easy, it was her.

ELIZABETH. Clarissa?!

CLARISSA (*to* RICHARD). Arrrrrre youuuuu serious?

RICHARD. Seven thousand Twitter followers, right? Let she who's without sin post the first tweet.

CLARISSA. You put me up to it!

RICHARD. Me? I don't even use Twitter.

CLARISSA. You evil little devil-fucking shit-scarfing *LIAR*.

ELIZABETH. Okay I've heard enough. This dance is over. Lights up, everybody outta here, NOW.

Everyone starts to scatter.

Not you Clarissa.

Everyone exits. ANNE *enters on another part of the stage. She's carrying a bucket. The scene shifts around her.*

ANNE (*to audience*). Hi there.
I know this is Richard's story so I'll be out of your way in a minute, but…
Funny how it's always Richard's story.
Or not Richard's but, you know. Hamlet's. Or Henry the VIII's. Or Eddie's. Or Tom's.

She puts down the bucket. RICHARD *enters in another part of the stage.*

RICHARD. So that got a bit out of hand, but once I explain my position I… what are you doing?

ANNE. If this were my story? It'd be about how I always kept
my head down, and waited. Just waited patiently, and
survived, and then left this place.
Because this is not me. This is not who I am.
I am not some idiot girl who got pregnant and everyone...
everyone knows.
I am not the kind of person who stupidly misplaces her trust.

RICHARD. Anne stop that.

ANNE (*urgent*). I'm not some small-town girl in a small-
minded town.
I'm not someone who keeps refreshing her phone to an
endless social media feed of taunts and barbs and reminders
of all of the idiot things that I've done. I'm not a tossed-off
afterthought like in a Shakespeare play where the ladies are
all a bunch of objects and character foils and plot devices.

*She pulls a washcloth out of the bucket, which is a bucket
of blood.*

I am not that person. I am above all that.
I'm a professional dancer. (*She streaks one forearm
with blood.*)
I'm a famous choreographer. (*She streaks the other forearm
with blood.*)
I'm soaring above the floorboards at Lincoln Center.
(*She wrings blood on her dress.*)
I'm not a stupid lonely girl with no options.
I'm not locked in my bathroom holding a box cutter.
I'm... I have agency. (*She displays her wrists.*)

I'm above the fray...
You're right in the fray.
I'm above petty gossip...
You are the gossip.
I am free...
You are chained.

The stage goes red. ANNE *drops the washcloth.*

Sorry. So sorry. This isn't my story.
I'll go now, I'll go.
In a minute I'll be out of your way.

She drifts off. RICHARD *looks at the spotlight of space she once occupied.*

RICHARD. I. I didn't. This isn't my fault. Look, I never meant for her to take it this far... This. This can't be happening. It's not real, this is not even real!

His mourning is interrupted by voice-overs and projections of tweets.

VOICE-OVER. @annemargaret such a tragedy

RICHARD. Wait.

VOICE-OVER. @annemargaret Rest in Peace

RICHARD. Wait, stop.

VOICE-OVER. I can't believe that you're gone @annemargaret.

RICHARD. Just shut up and give me a minute to *think*.

VOICE-OVER. Richard you were good to her.

VOICE-OVER. Richard you tried to defend her.

RICHARD. I what?

VOICE-OVER. Richard?

VOICE-OVER. Richard?

VOICE-OVER. All hail Richard! Richard is good!

RICHARD. I'm *not*!

VOICE-OVER (*a slow chant*). Richard is good. Richard is good.

The tweets devolve into a pep rally chant of 'Richard is good, Richard is good!' The stage rains down a shower of 'I Voted' stickers that float down on the audience like confetti.

Scene Nine – Bare Stage

Before he can recover ELIZABETH *enters elsewhere on stage.*

ELIZABETH (*whispering*). Richard. *Richard.*

RICHARD. What? *What*?! Not now.

ELIZABETH. Richard your speech.

RICHARD. My what?

A podium invades the scene.

ELIZABETH. Your acceptance speech, Richard go!

RICHARD. Oh my… oh, oh. (*Direct address.*) I stand before
you as president weighted by leaden spirits. Elected. But not
with any relish in it. Believe me, I never wanted to get here
this way. But with Eddie on a leave of absence and no other
candidates on the ballot, it seems I've been thrust this
election by virtue of a most unfortunate fortune. Doubtless
you're aware of what's befallen Anne Margaret… my
girlfriend. That dazzling ray of sunlight, sun-setted by the
tenebrosity in our own dark hearts.

For make no mistake: we did this to her. The football team's
culture of recklessness and impunity. All of your gossip,
your judging, your voracious need for an online stoning of
her. Well you did it. You killed her.

Many of you may not know that the president holds the
power of the purse strings over this school. Well it's my
intention to make full use of that power, on Anne's behalf.
Anne loved to dance. It was her dream to 'go professional' in
New York City. For that reason, I will construct a dance
studio here in her name. We are going to save the arts!
Naturally these expenditures will require some rebalancing
in our bloated and wasteful school budget. The football team.
Is defunded. The computer lab is shut down. And no more
phones in here, got it? If I see so much as one cellphone –
one little tweet – I'm gonna go apeshit.

I think you all need to step back and think about what you've
done to that poor girl. And for that matter what you've done

to people like *me*. Treated us like we're invisible. To be stepped on. Well I'm here. I'm here and I am your goddam *president* and I am not to be trifled with.

Lights shift and BUCK *enters before* RICHARD *can recover.*

BUCK. Nice speech.

RICHARD. *What?*

BUCK. I said nice speech ya creepy dictator. What, did ya look up clips of Mussolini on YouTube?

RICHARD. It was somewhat impromptu. How long've you been here?

BUCK. Well congratulations. You got exactly what you wanted.

RICHARD. I didn't want this.

BUCK. Oh really. Eddie's on leave, Clarissa's transferring schools, and here *you are* with no dirt on your shoes and a clear path to the presidency. Who cares about *Anne* though.

RICHARD. She made her decision, that wasn't me.

BUCK. *Richard*, of course it's on you. Admit that you killed her.

RICHARD. Killed my own girlfriend?? How can you say that to me?

BUCK. I don't want to believe you'd play God with Anne for a stupid election. But fuck Richard: it *sounds* like you. So don't lie about it okay? Just don't run a scheme on *me*!

RICHARD. I'm not.

BUCK. Then tell me the truth, you owe me that much.

RICHARD. No one owes anyone shit. You taught me that. And if you've got a problem with it, why don't you *stand up* and say something.

BUCK. *Richard*.

RICHARD. No, I'm sick of you trying to perch on my shoulder acting like the voice of conscience, you got that Jiminy *Crippet*? You think being Eddie's lackey's gonna earn you

his love? He'd never touch you. You will wither in that chair
alone and unloved because that is the only reward for being
a pining sycophant toad. <u>You want my confession? Yeah fine</u>,
<u>I planned allll of this.</u> But here's the rub you dumb weasel:
from down there you can't do a thing.

BUCK. Actually I just did.

EDDIE. HEY! (*Enters.*) You're a *fuckin' asshole*.

RICHARD. Eddie? No WAIT Eddie, WAIT!

BUCK *exits as* EDDIE *tackles* RICHARD, *and just beats the
shit out of him. I mean just kicks the ever-loving shit out of
the guy.*

EDDIE. THAT's for Annie, you prick. And this is for Buck.

EDDIE *kicks him.* ELIZABETH *enters.*

ELIZABETH. Omigod Richard! *Richard?!* Are you okay?

EDDIE. I hope not. I hope the prick never walks. (*He exits.*)

ELIZABETH. Eddie? Eddie, get back here!

RICHARD. Buck! Buck has betrayed me!

ELIZABETH. No, no, honey don't try to move. What the hell
was that? And what the hell was that speech? Richard I thought
you and I had an understanding. I thought I was mentoring
you! I just, I thought you were one of the good ones!

RICHARD. Yeah well. I'm not your saint and I'm not your
dead brother, so it looks like you're not the savior you
thought you were.

ELIZABETH (*hurt*). You're just in pain. I'll go get the nurse.
(*She exits.*)

RICHARD. Ah, Buck. Buck has betrayed me. But not before
teaching me this.

He does a weird hand gesture thing and produces
ELIZABETH's *keys. Spotlight on* RICHARD *as he stands
and the lights shift.*

And then suddenly I'm shambling to my feet again. And I'm in the parking lot. And then suddenly I find myself behind the steering wheel of a car for the very first time. A thunderous, galloping SUV. A chariot fit for a king.

And then there he is. Eddie. My unfoilable foil.

And in that moment I think: Is this all there is to having the keys to the kingdom? And in that moment, I think: I've got Eddie's job, but do I have Eddie's *hide*? And in that moment, I think: my kingdom for some *horsepower*. And then the next moment my foot's on the gas pedal.

Lights up on EDDIE. *He squints in the headlights.*

EDDIE. What the fuck…?

ELIZABETH, CLARISSA, *and* BUCK *enter*.

CLARISSA. Oh my gosh what is he doing?

BUCK. Stop stop stop!

ELIZABETH. Richard, NO!

All is frozen. ANNE *enters as an apparition. Maybe she's in a bloodied white version of the dress she wore at the dance. She and* RICHARD *meet eyes.*

ANNE. Hey asshole: don't do this.

RICHARD. I have to.

ANNE. *You don't*. Richard, you've won.

RICHARD. And what have I won *exactly*. If he can swoop down in an instant and rob me of standing, of your memory, of my love. Rob me of my very *body*, dispossess me of all that I own. What can I ever hope to win, Anne. Except my revenge.

ANNE. Richard: this isn't you.

RICHARD. *I don't care!* Like you know me so well.

ANNE. I'd like to think I was getting there. But then again maybe I don't know you, because fool that I am I thought I meant something to you. But congrats on the election. Hope it was worth my life.

RICHARD. I didn't kill you! I never meant for you to get hurt.

ANNE. Richard would you take some goddam *responsibility*? For once? Look at us: Buck, and Clarissa, and me? These are your friends. Supposedly.

RICHARD. So then what, I'm the villain? He's the real villain. You just want to protect him again.

ANNE. *Hey lunkhead* it's you I'm protecting, not him. Don't throw away your future over some petty revenge thing!

RICHARD. But then he gets away with it. Again. He goes on to live his dumb perfect life and I am stuck in *this life*, I am stuck.

ANNE. And yet I did love you.

RICHARD. I can't even... No, Anne, I'll never believe that.

ANNE. Then that is what makes you the villain.

RICHARD. Oh that is so easy for you to say that, you know that Anne? You with all the privileges and advantages in the world, by all means muster the gall to tell me to rise up from my circumstance.

ANNE. All the *advantages*? Richard: I'm dead.

RICHARD. Hush, gentle spirit, you're not even real. You're but an apparition of idealized beauty, all my remorse corporealized out of guilt pangs and dust. Loved me? What does it matter whether you loved me. Strumpet. A termagant, you. Now back to the shadows, shade, and prick not my conscience again.

He turns to the audience as she fades away.

I'm sorry where were we? Oh that's right.

Lights shift and the engine revs.

ELIZABETH. Richard, NO!

Car sound! EDDIE *falls.*

EDDIE. Ahhh!

RICHARD. And that's when I run Eddie over. First the front wheels then the back. Severing his spinal cord between the L1 and L2 vertebrae, never to walk again.

EDDIE. I can't feel my legs, I can't feel my legs…

RICHARD. Now who's the cripple?

ELIZABETH. Richard. What have you done?

RICHARD. The only thing left to do. ~~You already decided who I was before it was mine to choose it, so what else could I do but act out the role that's been writ? If that makes me the~~ *villain,* ~~welllll… You already knew I wasn't the hero from the moment I came limping your way.~~ So close your eyes and forget about me. You always do anyhow.

Lights out. Lights up again and he's gone. The remaining actors look at the negative space for a moment, then curtain call.

End of Play.

Alternative Lines

The following alternative lines can be substituted so that Richard's character has cerebral palsy instead of hemiplegia. (These are the only authorized substitutions that can be made in the script.)

—

Page 20

ELIZABETH. Richard did I ever tell you I had a brother who was disabled?

RICHARD. Did he have ~~hemiplegia~~ **cerebral palsy** like me?

—

Page 25

RICHARD. Or do you fear me? Are you scared you might ~~be paralyzed~~ **contract cerebral palsy** just by the taint of my touch?

—

Page 28

BUCK. You can't call me that! You have fucking ~~hemiplegia~~ **CP**.

—

Page 34

ANNE. / you have a great range of motion on the left, I can totally work with that

RICHARD. Oh yeah, um, okay.

ANNE. But unfortunately ~~your right side's~~ **you're also** a little bit spazzy, which is gonna be harder to work with.

—

Page 36

ANNE.…Put the ~~arm~~ **arms** down! Relax…

—

Page 37

ANNE.…If that's too much to ask I'm sorry.

RICHARD. No, it's fine, I've never been asked… **You know how sometimes in winter when you hit an ice patch you didn't know was there, how you brace yourself before you're about to slip on the ice?**

ANNE. **Yeah…**

RICHARD. **That's what it's like for me all the time. My muscles and nerves are fine. It's just my brain is in constant winter-ice mode, sending out panic signals like at any moment I'm right about to fall down. Which in some moments is actually true.**

ANNE. **You know but before you started fucking around you were doing okay.** Dancing – at least this kind of fake-ass school-dance dancing – it's less about fast motion and just – (*She approaches*.) – Can I?

—

Page 43

RICHARD. Ahhhh. Nooooo. Noooooo!

~~EDDIE. Yo fuck are you wearing a diaper??~~

~~RICHARD. Fuck you!~~

EDDIE. ~~That is so Fucked Up. Here's some advice big baby:~~ Do not. (*Pull!*)

RICHARD. Ahh watch the balls —

—

Page 47

RICHARD. Ahhhh but it is though. It's extremely weird down there. ~~I'm not even sure what all works.~~

~~ANNE. Shall we have a look and find out?~~

~~RICHARD. Yeah okay but just to be — just, full disclosure? I'm wearing a diaper. You were going to find out anyway so there it is Anne. I'm an adult diaper wearer. Does that repulse you, that I'm a big baby, or is that your kink? I'm pretty sure that's nobody's kink. I should leave.~~

~~ANNE. Hey nobody asked for that. Richard? Calm the fuck down.~~

~~RICHARD. Oh my God I am just. I've got diarrhea of the mouth don't I, the diaper should be on my face.~~

ANNE. Let's just. Enter this. With no preconceptions.

www.nickhernbooks.co.uk

facebook.com/nickhernbooks

twitter.com/nickhernbooks